British Library Cataloguing in Publication Data

Wood, Jakki
In the park.
1. Great Britain. Parks
I. Title II. Series
941.085'8

ISBN 0–340–50233–9

First published 1989

Published by Hodder and Stoughton Children's Books,
a division of Hodder and Stoughton Ltd
Mill Road, Dunton Green, Sevenoaks Kent TN13 2YA

Printed in Belgium by Proost International Book Production

In the Park

by Jakki Wood

HODDER AND STOUGHTON
LONDON SYDNEY AUCKLAND TORONTO

One warm spring afternoon Alex and Peter take Judy for a walk in the park.

'Oh look,' cries Peter, 'there's Sam and Sarah.'

Industrial towns and cities were once smoky, dirty and dark. Parks were created to give working people the chance to enjoy some fresh air and light.

The children have brought some brown bread to feed the birds. Judy is so greedy she wants some, too.

‘Oh Judy, don’t do that,’ shouts Alex.

All kinds of birds are busy at this time of year, building nests and looking for food for their young.

Starling

Chaffinch

Pigeon

Collared dove

House sparrow

Tree sparrow

The fluffy young blue tits leave the nest at the end of April. They stay together as a family for the first few weeks.

Birch catkins grow in April and stay on the tree until autumn. They then break up into winged wind-borne seeds.

'Here Judy, fetch,' calls Peter as he throws the ball. Sarah and Alex watch a family of young blue tits being fed in a birch tree.

Judy dashes off towards a huge rhododendron bush.

'Oh no! She's going to hide the ball,' says Peter.

'Judy, come back, you bad dog.'

Spring flowers provide nectar for insects such as bees and butterflies, which emerge in early spring after a long hibernation.

The beautiful pink-white flowers of some magnolia trees come out before the leaves.

Brimstone butterfly

Honey-bee

◄ *Bumble-bee*

It is dark and quiet under the bush. Judy frightens a sleepy hedgehog, which quickly rolls up into a ball. Judy is so surprised she just sits and stares.

Hedgehogs sleep through the coldest winter days until the spring, when they wake up and begin to look for food. They also sleep during the day, coming out at dusk to hunt for worms, slugs and snails.

When a hedgehog is startled, it rolls up into a ball. Its sharp spines protect it from its enemies.

Garden snail

Slug

'Come on Judy,' calls Peter. Judy runs back to the children, straight over a flower-bed.

'Naughty girl,' scolds Alex. 'I hope the park-keeper didn't see you!'

In spring, green shoots begin to appear. In parks, where flower-beds are changed often, gardeners plant out the flower-beds a few weeks before they want flowers. In gardens, most flowering plants blossom year after year.

'Shh! Look, squirrels,' says Sarah. 'They're digging under that tree.' Alex quickly grabs Judy so that she can't chase them away.

Grey squirrels were brought to Great Britain from North America over 100 years ago. They spread quickly and soon became much more common than the smaller, timid red squirrels. Today, red squirrels are usually found only in remote areas of Britain.

'The squirrels have been eating the seeds in these pine cones, too,' Mum says. But the boys don't hear. They have run off to a horse chestnut tree nearby.

Squirrels gnaw at pine cones to reach the seeds hidden between the scales of the cones.

Like many insects, the Peacock butterfly hibernates during the winter.

Horse chestnut flowers

By the time the spring comes, some of last autumn's seeds have germinated. The seed case splits open and a thin root grows down into the soil. Then a tiny green shoot begins to grow upwards towards the light.

Lesser celandine

Primrose

‘Let’s see if there are any conkers left from last year,’ says Peter.

‘I’ve found one,’ says Sam ‘but it’s sprouted. I wonder if Judy will find any.’

The cherry trees near the pond are covered with beautiful pink and white blossoms.

'Don't go too near that swan, Judy!' warns Mum.

Mute swans are white, with a bright orange beak. In the spring, they make their nests in clumps of reeds. Their young are called cygnets, and have grey/brown feathers. Adult swans can be very aggressive when they have young, so it's best not to get too close.

Japanese cherry blossoms

Many of the ducks and geese in parks are introduced ornamental varieties. The large flight feathers at the tips of their wings are clipped to stop them flying away. Female ducks usually have a duller colouring.

Mandarin male

Mandarin female

Teal

Tufted duck

Red-crested pochard

Alex has saved some of the bread.

'Here ducks,' she calls.

'Oh, look at that one. It's got red hair!' laughs Peter. Judy stays well away.

'That's all,' says Alex. 'There's no more bread now.'

'Come on,' says Mum. 'It's our tea-time, too. Put Judy back on the lead.'

They all walk back to the park gates, and on home.

You can see Canada geese on ponds, lakes and rivers. When a large number of geese live together, the goslings (young geese) are herded into a nursery, where they are looked after by two or more adults.

INDEX